In The Artist's Words
An Interview with CW Mundy
By Linda Riesenberg Fisler

Table of Contents

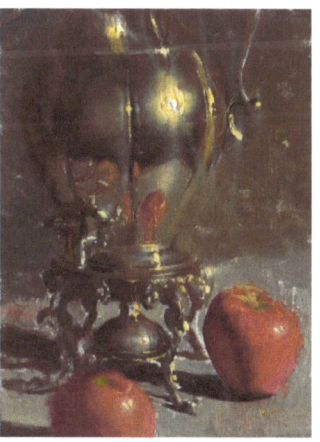

2011 Silver Coffee Urn, oil on linen, 12x9
©CWMundy SOLD Permanent Collection Indiana Heritage Arts

Foreword: Recollections from our time on the Air

By Linda Riesenberg Fisler

On June 12, 2012, Blanche McAlister Harris and I had a wonderful time interviewing CW Mundy.   We covered a lot of topics in this 90 minute interview. Everything from how opportunities for travel present themselves(or do they?); to his experience taking Sherrie McGraw's drawing class and what he thinks about Sherrie; to not just painting shapes but to incorporate form into those shapes; to being fearless when you paint; to his music pursuits! I could go on and on, but then this would be the longest foreword ever and you wouldn't need the transcripts!

Being an artist, CW told us, you "need to go where your heart is and where the passion is. You make these opportunities happen and if you sit around and wait for somebody to rescue you and come up with an idea, if that is what is going on with you as an artist, you are in the wrong profession."   I can't emphasize this enough. I can't tell you how many successful Master artists have told me this. Want to get into a gallery? CW's answer is very much the same and I quote him here…."It's the same thing with a gallery… 'I'm going to be discovered'…ain't gonna happen. You need to make it happen."

We asked CW to tell us about his recent experience taking Sherrie McGraw's drawing workshop. CW had the highest praise for Sherrie and talked about how important it is that shapes have form. "In my estimation, Sherrie McGraw is one of the best draftsman in the country and maybe one of the finest draftsman in the world. She got that from really paying attention to Dave Leffel and David really taught her the shorthand of drawing." CW went on to say that he was taught to measure everything and he *has* taught to measure everything. Since he attended Sherrie's workshop, his approach has changed. The transcript provides more insight on why.

Here's the thing with CW, he considers himself still learning. We consider CW a Master and rightfully so, and he has "it". But his openness to learning from his peers really comes through during this interview and if we walk away with only one learning (which is virtually impossible to do), it is that all through our artist career we need to be learning not only from present day Master artists, but our peers, from past masters and from exploring in our studios (whether inside or outside). It is a part of what keeps us inspired, keeps us from getting bored and keeps us coming back to paint again. And just as important is getting your ego out of the way so that you are open to learning.

I can remember only hearing of CW from other Master artists and artists. I can remember before meeting him that I was a bit fearful of him, his presence. CW is larger than life, but a truly loving human being. He admits to being opinionated and he will gladly provide his opinion anytime. But CW will listen to you and will genuinely try to help you become a better painter, starting you on your way to becoming a better artist. Don't know the difference? Don't worry, it's in the transcript. And now, to this day, I can honestly say that I wish I would have met CW a long time ago. The fear has been replaced with appreciation of his work, work ethic, his knowledge and love for this kind-hearted soul. He is fun-loving, a joker, and yet at a drop of a hat can be dead serious. I love every bit of this man, his wife Rebecca and what they stand for because they do it honestly.

We had a discussion on being fearless. You may never find your voice if you don't hang out on the edge. You may be painting wonderful paintings, but they may also be boring.   "You must know the science and have the knowledge, you cannot march up the ladder … if you ignore the science…you have to know this (the science) and then spinning it in a very creative way."   When you have the knowledge and understand the science most of us become fearful. The paintings become too precious. We become timid about ruining what we have. CW encourages us to put that fear aside and "hang out there really far left or far right because that is where an artist discovers…"

I hope you approach this transcript/eBook with the same ferocity that you attack a canvas. Grab a pen and highlighter. Write down your ah-has and what inspires you. Highlight phrases that make you want to go paint. Take a marker and write them on paper to hang in your studio. Take the transcript with you in the field to read when you are finding that the painting is too precious to explore. Remember to destroy it and build it back. Hang out on the edge just a little bit and see how much of an artist you become. I've spent many, many hours creating this eBook and I can honestly say that there are a number of key phrases that keep me exploring in my time behind the easel. Some I have quoted here. Some are still buried in the transcript and mean something that I have yet to discover. For each time I re-visit this eBook/interview, I find something new that I didn't see before. I hope this is true for you.

It's about the journey, so keep walking.

Linda Riesenberg Fisler

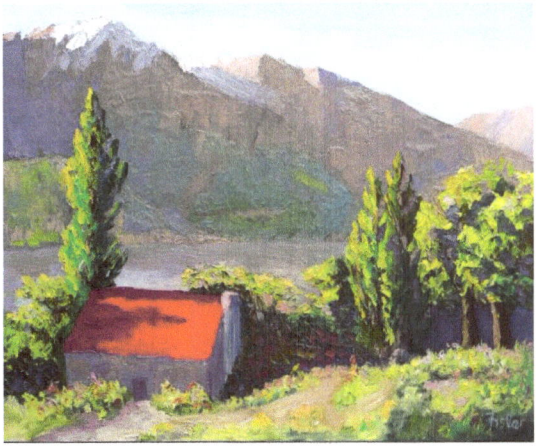

My first hanging out on the limb painting-exploring!

©Linda Riesenberg Fisler Little Red Cottage, 16 x 20, Oil on Canvas,
 Sold, In the collection of Julie & George Gallo

Linda: Hi everyone and welcome to AMO Art Chat. We have a great show tonight. CW Mundy is with us. I just wanted to make a couple of quick announcements. Next week on June 21st we actually have one of our regularly scheduled shows. And that will be with Wayne Johnson who is a musician and a friend of mine. We'll be talking about Investigating the Creative Process. Wayne is a musician, just like CW is, so you are actually going to get a foreshadowing of that show this evening as we talk to CW about his music a little bit later on this evening as well. The Chat window is open so if you are listening with us live please feel free to log into the chat window and if you have any questions during the show please post them in the chat window and we'll try to get them on the air. There is also a number at the top of the screen for guest call in. I'm not going to promise if you call that number that I'll get you on the air but if you would like to try, that is fine, it just depends on how the conversation is going, whether I can get to you or not. Your best way of getting questions to us is actually do it through the chat window. It is a lot easier for me to kind of keep up with everybody logged in on the chat window than it is to go back and forth on the phones. Let me introduce our co-host and then we'll get right to CW because we have a lot to talk about tonight.

Linda: Blanche McAlister Harris is with us tonight. Hello Blanche.

Blanche: Hi Linda How are you doing?

Linda: I'm doing pretty well. I actually got to the studio to paint a little bit today. Got rid of the blues. How about you?

Blanche: Oh, I'm doing well. I have been trying to get to my studio. Going through reference photos and getting ready to start a new painting maybe tomorrow if all goes well.

Linda: Yeah I'm going to get back into the studio tomorrow while the paint is still wet, so I can work wet into wet. So I think we are in the same boat. (Laughter) Yeah. Ok, well, I want to get right to CW because there are a lot of folks calling in and want to hear him more than they want to hear us.

CW is an impressionist artist. He is living in Indianapolis, born and raised in Indiana. He actually attended Ball State University graduating with a Bachelor of Fine Arts. Then he traveled out to California where he painted and played music. He worked on his Master of Fine Arts degree at Long Beach State. Then in 1978, he returned home to Indiana and worked as a sports illustrator for a decade and then in the early 1990s took on the challenge of painting in a more impressionistic way, going out of doors and painting en plein air from life. He had a number of trips to Europe and that began back in 1995 when he traveled to France. He still travels overseas today. In 2007, he achieved Masters Status with the American Impressionist Society and we actually have some questions from our fellow members at the American Impressionist Society as part of our show tonight so we'll actually highlight when we ask their questions. Then in 2003 he was invited to Master Signature status in the Oil Painters of America group. He is a signature member American Society of Marine Artists. Welcome CW. How are you tonight?

CW: I'm doing great girls! It's exciting to be here and let's get to it, baby. I've got a slogan. It is a hillbilly colloquial. I'll treat you a whole bunch of different ways. You're bound to like one of them.

Linda: (Laughing) Ok, well, I'll tell you what. I'm going to throw it to Blanche who is going to ask you the first question. We are going to actually start talking a little bit about your travels. Go ahead, Blanche.

Blanche: CW, I saw on your website that you just returned from Massachusetts, where you were painting. You said it is one of your favorite places to paint. Why do you like Massachusetts so much?

CW: It is not so much about Massachusetts, but it is Gloucester, Rockport, its harbors. I love the old dirty fishing villages. The blue collar places where they are actually working and doing it as a career and making money instead of floating around in the Clorox bottles, the real expensive white yachts with the perfect white sails and all the golden necklaces and all that stuff. I like the blue collar places. Gloucester has great history. You know, there were a host of painters that painted there at the turn of the century. Anthony Thieme, Emile Gruppe, Frederick Mulhaupt, Willard Metcalf, and I think Twachtman painted out there just to name a few. So, it's just got a great heritage.

Blanche: What are some of your other favorite spots to paint?

CW: Everywhere! (Laughs) No actually, there's so many different...I love Europe. You know you'd have to be brain dead to go over to Europe and not find something to paint. This is probably the greatest, the only good thing about socialism, that happened to Europe and that is they still have the old buildings and they have all the history that we don't have in our buildings. You know you build a building in America and 50 years later you have to tear it down because the real estate is worth more than the building. So back then--there is just so much antiquity, beautiful sculpture, and beautiful architecture. I'm just in love with Europe. I love Europe. I can't get enough of it. And there are great places all across this wonderful country to paint too. You know, we like to go out West. We like the Midwest. We have these big overcast days that the California Plein Air painters don't want to paint because they have to have light and shadow. But talk to Dan Gerhartz or myself, and you get an opulence day, a cloudy grey day and you can really set a mood in a painting and it not just this bright light shadow that all the California plein air painters think they have to have to paint.

Linda: Are you going over to Europe any time soon?

CW: Well, we were thinking about maybe going back again to France or Italy. We've got some time slots that we left open this year. We pray about everything and if we feel we get moved to go in one direction or the other, then we do that. We don't like to stick ourselves in a box. I'm very careful about making commitments because you have to keep your commitments and that can really mess up a chance to all the sudden, say, "Hey, we feel lead. Let's take off to Europe. Let's go somewhere and paint or do something." you know...so…

Blanche: You want to leave yourself free to travel.

CW: Yeah, yeah you want to leave those slots open as much as you can.

Linda: It is kind of interesting. You know I work with Kevin Macpherson and we were talking before the show. One of the things that I have always asked Kevin, because he travels a lot as well, and doesn't like a lot commitments so that he can just pick up and go to his new favorite place, which is China, but I always ask he how gets all these different opportunities to travel. And one of the things he has said, is that he makes his own opportunities and I'm assuming that is true with you. You just don't have someone calling you up and saying "Hey, we want you to go over and paint twenty paintings of some place in France." But you actually go make those opportunities to travel for yourself. Is that correct?

CW: Oh yes, I do not need anybody to invent ideas for me. You know, I have a hard enough problem investigating all the things I can creatively come up with. I have turned down projects where they wanted me to be involved in a book or something like that because you have to go paint in these locations and that is not what an artist needs to do. He needs to go where his heart is and where his passion is and where he feels lead to go and do it. I don't really want anybody else's idea. I've got enough of my own and that is the same thing with Kevin. And you make these opportunities happen. You don't sit around and wait for somebody to rescue you and come up with an idea. If that is what is going on with you as an artist you are probably in the wrong profession.

Linda: I have heard that so much from so many different artists that I think that is such great advice for everybody who paints. If you want to go to France, then go to France and paint. Don't wait for somebody to tell you to go to France and paint. You make your own opportunities don't wait for them to come to you.

Blanche: You got to make it happen.

Linda: Right.

CW: It is the same thing with the galleries. People are waiting. They think, "Well I'll, you know, I'm going to be discovered." (buzzer sound) Negatory! Not going to happen. Wouldn't be prudent. You gotta make, ah, your career happen. You've got to do it and don't leave it up to somebody else. You know, I thank the Lord about that. He's given us the wisdom. My wife, Rebecca, is not only my wife, but the most important business partner in this whole CW Mundy Fine Art thing. We are progressive with everything. We take everything under consideration.

We do logical things that will give us the attention we need to become the trade name--to become all that we've been able to become. In the industry you'll not become the trade name in the industry if you don't take control of your career. It is one thing to paint and it is one thing to launch your career. But it is a whole other thing to sustain it and you have to be fully responsible. That's one of the things I teach in my workshops. For those who are painting to have a career, I spend about two and half hours and I tell them my whole story and tell them they are no different. And if they really are serious there are prudent things that you need to do. I'm grateful that God gave me that business sense. You know you just can't sit around and paint great paintings if nobody can see them. And if you don't get the right publicity and if you don't put yourself out there in front of the market than nobody is going to know about you, you'll be a shelf artist the rest of your career. It is an important thing to do. There is a balance there. You have to continue to paint but you also have to do that business end. That is where I'm fortunate because I have my wife to do that. In fact, when we started the fine art thing, our gallery manager and my wife told me: "Look we'll take care of everything in the business that we need to take care of and you do what you can do and you paint." And I'm so grateful. Because believe me, the amount of people who come and take my workshop and the majority of these people are women and they don't have a spouse to do this, because their spouse is working and playing golf. They don't have somebody like I'm so fortunate to have: a wife and a partner that does all of that. And of course, I get to be in the decision making too. But, you know, it does, it takes a lot of energy and a lot time and effort. So believe me I know I'm very grateful and very blessed at what my wife Rebecca does. Otherwise I wouldn't have a career.

Blanche: The business side takes so much time. A lot of people don't realize that.

CW: Yes ma'am.

Blanche: CW, I wanted to ask you a question that I have gotten from Ellie, who is a member of the American Impressionist Society. She wanted me to ask you what your take away was from your recent trip, well, the recent class you attended with Sherrie McGraw on drawing. I think it was in Connecticut?

CW: Oh man! I could spend the rest of the program talking about that. I mean this as serious a statement that I can make about anything. In my estimation, Sherrie McGraw is probably one of the finest draftsman I know in the country and maybe one of the finest draftsman in the world. She got that from really paying attention to David (Leffel) and David really taught her the shorthand of drawing and she worked very hard at it. She has one of the most beautiful graceful styles and I was able to see that. And then I bought her book and after I bought her book and read it, I was very interested because I grew up and my education in drawing was measuring. Measuring one thing against another, measuring one thing against another and that is what I've been teaching for 20 years. All the sudden I run into Sherrie and find out that is not what you really want to do. The problem with that is that you left brain everything to death and she made a comment, you know the classical realist will spend 300 hours on a 30x20 drawing of the figure and when they are done with it they have a very stiff boring, no form or movement in the form what so ever. A static drawing that will bore you to death. And if you look at Michelangelo, Peter Paul Rubens, Fechin, Rembrandt, da Vinci and you see these masters and see how they were able to--form overlaps form and that is the way of foreshortening by signaling that in the drawing and the other tips that she has, that she gleaned from David, I'm speaking of David Leffel and his study and research and you are pulling from the greatest of the greatest. And I was so amazed that I found out these things that I really had no handle on and was not doing in my career: getting that beautiful form and the movement of the form. It is one thing to see a shape, and that's what you need to do. That is the foundation of every good painting. You've got to identify the value shapes and the shapes and how they are relating to each other but on top of that the next big thing is that you've got to understand the form of that shape. Then once you are able to get the gesture of that shape and the gesture of that form, you are home free, baby! Now your art's going to have a thread of what the greatest masters that have ever created had and that what's, I tell ya, as I said, I could talk--the whole show could be what I learned from Sherrie McGraw and how much I love her and respect her and how grateful I am and because how influential she was to me...I've already done my first two painting since I've been back and they have movement and that form and that understanding of the overlapping form that the masters did to show mass and how to show movement and everything and so I'm just like a....I don't know, I don't know what expression to say other than to say I'm so grateful, I'm like a kid at Christmas.

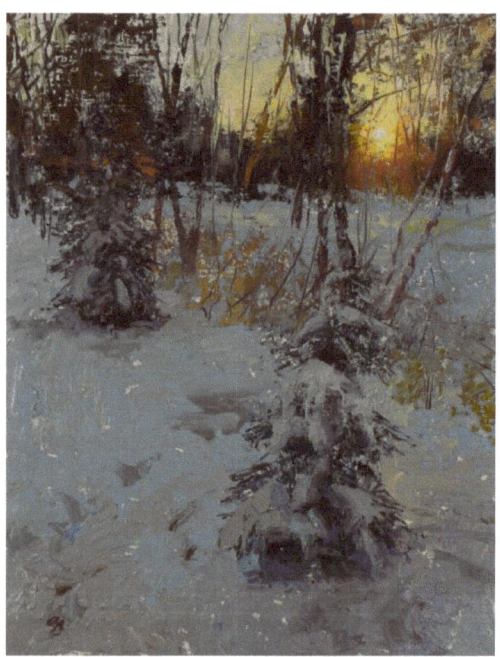

Sunrise, My Back Yard, oil on linen, 20x16
©CWMundy 2013

Linda: It sounds like you had an Ah-Ha moment there. I mean, it…

CW: Yes I did! It was like a major epiphany. And when you can say what I'm saying, believe me I'm not just saying as my father said, I'm not just whistling Dixie. I mean it and Sherrie knows I mean it. I've said to her and in front of the class--we did a dual demo, and I told every artist there.."You know what every brand name out there in the industry and I'm talking about the big boys and the big girls-and everybody else that is doing art needs to take her drawing class because it will take them to a whole new level that they cannot even fathom." And I told Sherrie two thirds through the class, I said you know what, I'm changed and I don't know how this is going to work, but I know that I'm going be able to apply this. I apply it to my landscape, to my still life. I apply to painting even though drawing and painting are two different mediums. I'm going to be a whole lot better artist---I already am…because of Sherrie McGraw's class.

Blanche: Wow!! That's exciting!

CW: That's a plug for her and I love her. She couldn't be a sweeter, nicer person.

Blanche: Sounds like a lot of us need to look into that. It's a whole new approach.

CW: Oh yes. It will wake you up. When you think about it, think about this, you are using the most important stuff we've been able to glean from the history of art, from the greatest artists that ever lived. You know it is pretty interesting how part of my quest was--everybody talks about well you know--everybody is looking at Sargent and everybody is looking at Zorn and everybody is looking at Sorolla and you hear their names mentioned and rightly so because those guys are masters, don't get me wrong, but who did they look to? They looked to Peter Paul Rubens, Michelangelo, Rembrandt. And I'll tell you another discovery that just blew my mind on this quest. I answered my own question and that is what I answer when everybody is talking about these guys--but who did these guys admire, Velazquez! I looked at him and I looked at a few other artists and what was amazing because everybody knows I'm an edge freak and when I finally got to Rembrandt I was so blown away, because Rembrandt was the guy that took more liberties with edges than any other major, famous artist, important artist in history that I know of. He took more liberties with edge work and that is what I love, because you know edges are one of the foundational tenants of the science of painting. He took a lot of liberties and so I'm really on the other extreme from ultra conservatives that say you know, "Oh God forbid, don't make up anything. All you have to do is see." Well that is the beginning part. Yeah, you've got to see what is going on, but you need to paint the way you see. And that is a whole other story with edges when we see. The human being when he sees and he looks: if I were sitting in the booth with you guys and I am looking at Linda or Blanche and I'm looking at one of their faces I only see 15% is in focus and everything else is out of focus. Why? Because God made us that way, so we could have intelligent conversations and we could focus on what we need to focus. So that is the way you need to paint. You figure out what the center of focus is and you can have your strongest edge or strongest color, your heaviest paint, whatever, and you can anchor that in. What you want people to look at and everything else as it moves away from that becomes less and less important, knock the edges off and more out of focus less important- you know editing. And like George Gallo said, the biggest ball game in town is design and it is all about the directorship. I had a conversation with Gerhartz about a month and half before I went down to Florida this winter and I told Dan. I confessed to Dan. I've been,--I have to really confess, I have fallen asleep. With all the stuff that I know I can be so much better director and why am I not doing that? Why am I not being the director that I can be? Because that's the whole, that is what George was talking about, that is what it is. Think about it, the movie in Hollywood that wins best picture and wins the Oscar, guess who else wins the Oscar? The director. The point being is: your subject you have the most beautiful subject in front of you just like they can have Tom Cruise or Brad Pitt or whoever, great actors, great looking actresses, great script, great screenwriting, great music and if the directorship is C plus or B minus that movie is never going to be the number one--you know, the one that wins the Oscar. So it is the same thing with your painting. If you don't take on the responsibility of directing that subject the way it needs to be directed, then you are going to have mediocrity the rest of your life in painting. And that is why you need the science, which I know we're going to talk about later. I know I'm running off… I'm just going off on stuff that I find....you know what I want to tell the audience, Linda and Blanche, is the same thing I want to tell all my students. There is a real logical approach to this science of painting and the more logic that you have that gives you the more freedom and the more ability for the natural voice of who you are and who you can be as an artist to come out. You are only crippled if you do not understand the science of painting. You're totally crippled and you cannot march up the ladder in the industry and you cannot become the painter you can become if you ignore the science. You know, red is the complementary of green: blue is the complementary of orange: yellow is the complementary of purple. That is the way it is. That is the way the brain sees it. That is the way the history of art talks about it. That's a fact. And so painting is all about factual stuff and spinning it in a very creative way.

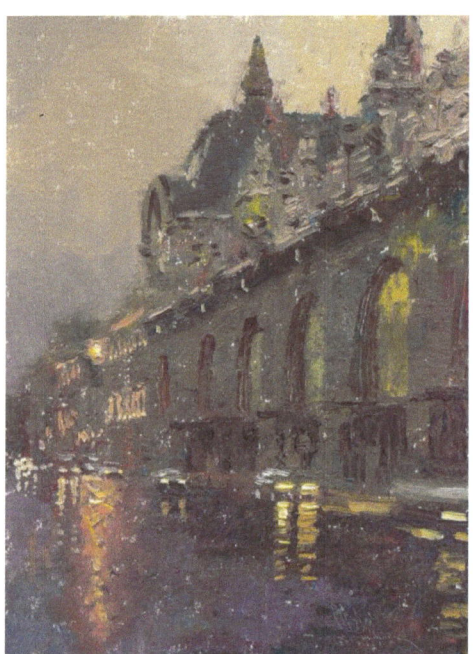

2012 - Musee D'Orsay, oil on linen, 12x9©CWMundy

Linda: CW, I want to take you back a second. You were talking about Rembrandt and I had the privilege of seeing "Rembrandt in America" down in North Carolina that was an exhibition where they had some Rembrandt's and some painting that were attributed to Rembrandt. And some of them were attributed falsely and they are in questions now. It was really interesting. I don't know Blanche that was down in your neck of the woods. Hopefully you got over to see it as well.

Blanche: I didn't see it myself I did hear about it.

Linda: Ok, so I was walking around spending a lot of time looking at the different ones and there were ones that they still have attributed to Rembrandt but I really questioned if they were because when you stand in front of a Rembrandt or even a Fechin for that matter and you look at the way they handle the edges and the way that they handle color and the design if you want to go back that far. It is just so much..it is just so magnificent! You just--I heard the story where David Leffel has actually looked at paintings and maybe it was Rembrandt, maybe have been somebody else, but actually got tears in his eyes because--and I heard this also of Richard Schmid-it is because they feel they have so much more to learn and they are not there. And hearing your Ah-ha moment from you is just so amazing and so reinforces that even at the level you are at, you are still growing, still challenging yourself and still learning.

Blanche: That is impressive!

CW: Oh yeah--I'll tell you, I'm going to take Laura Robb's class because I was one of the artists that brought her down to a First Brush of Spring that is in Southern Indiana. I got Carolyn Anderson to come down and teach. I taught this last year and I got Laura Robb to come. And the thing learned from her, even though I haven't taken her class, I heard it from the students, is her ability to use transparent color and this is one of the great things, beautiful parts of her paintings when she does the floral and she does china that transparent look because when you think Flowbleu that is a transparent wash that is going on an opaque white. And to create that with opaque paint I had an epiphany there. Well dummy--you know that's so logical and I'm thinking why didn't I think of that? I got to know Laura and I just think the world of her. She is a very sweet. She's got the left brain down. She knows the science. But she is very creative and uses the right side of her brain and she's one of those people I just love their work because it is so poetic and so I'm going to take, she doesn't know this yet, but I'm going to take her class because I want to sit under her and have her slap my hand and tell me--"O Yeah! Yeah! Yeah! Yeah! That's it! That's it! There you go! There ya go!!" you know because I'm going, like you said, if you ever think you got the handle on everything you are heading for the trash can. You know, there is so much to learn out there and it is so exciting and it is going to make us all better artists and you are an absolute fool if you don't take classes from the people that really understand what they are doing. I have seen so many people who have taken my classes, you know, how their careers have been launched because they paid attention. And they don't paint the way I paint. When I teach classes that is the last thing I want them to be involved in is how I paint. What I teach them is the science of painting and make sure they understand the science and then they go off and paint the way they feel lead to paint because that is what the market is looking for. They don't need another CW Mundy. They don't need another David Leffel, They don't need another Dan Gerhartz, Carolyn Anderson, Sherrie McGraw, whoever, whoever. The industry already has that. They are looking for--I was just on the phone with Carolyn Anderson today and I told her, I said I tell my students this-well I quote her all the time--I quote all the people I learned stuff from and give them credit. Carolyn says "I've seen that before. Show me something I haven't seen." Now there you go, girls! Now that's the search that we need to be on. To find some way to express something a little bit differently that people haven't seen it. And that is what launched my career because I mean I was scolded in the beginning because --oh he's using the Kleenex and scuffing the canvas with the Kleenex and he's the Kleenex King and all that. Well, I'll tell you what, it gave me a totally different identity than anybody else in the industry and it launched my career and I learned a lot about it because I'll tell you girls sometimes I'm a one ply Kleenex and sometimes I'm a two ply, and that is because that is what it requires. See what I mean? That all has to do with paint manipulation. If you are just going to paint your painting with a stupid, boring brush and everything is painted the same way. (Buzzer sound) Negatory! You got a boring looking painting. You need to make a variety of registrations on that canvas that you can with paint and still have it unified. Now you got something going, Baby!

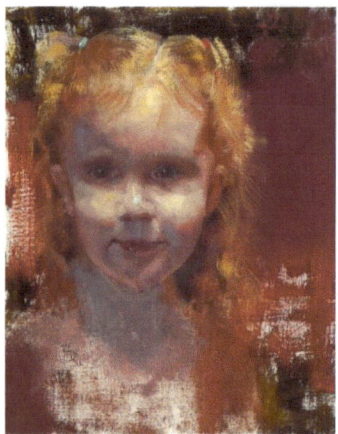

2011 - Melissa, oil on linen, 20x16 ©CWMundy
Awarded Jury Prize of Distinction For Portrait, Hoosier Salon 2011

Linda: I'm so glad you said that. I was painting today, you know I said that at the beginning and I got done basing in everything and said "Ok it's boring." So tomorrow afternoon we are going to take a palette knife to it and I'm going to see what I can do to it. At this point with the study that I have I want to start reaching out and exploring what I can do. And if it doesn't work, it doesn't work. I didn't lose anything. I learned something from it even if it is a failure.

CW: You are exactly right. Look, your failures, they will be the greatest teachers that you'll ever have because you'll know not to do it again. And I tell my student and say that to you, Linda and Blanche--listen you'll never know how far left is or how far right is until you go out and hang out on that edge. You can always come back to what the builders call Hoyle, you can always come back to a place that you feel comfortable with if you never ever venture out you never know that may be the sweet spot. Do you see what I mean? There are times when I'm out plein air painting and I have to put in a branch and so I just pick up a twig that is going to do it that is kind gnarly and scratchy on the end and I take that and scrape it right into wet paint. Bingo! If I would have done that with a paint brush. (buzzer sound) Boring! Too left brained! Not going to work! Taking your painting down a notch! So those are the things that with experience you learn because the biggest thing that I discuss and talk about is that the biggest problem that artists face because they don't have that adventurousness and don't have the confidence and so they end up left braining everything to death. And that is why they got a boring piece of artwork for people to look at because they left brain it to death. The problem is girls we are control freaks. Let's admit it. We're control freaks and if we get the chance we'll suck the blood out of everything. You have to know these things and when the sirens come up and (buzzer sound) it's boring--OK--then kick in the mode of being creative and go for it. You know one of the great things I learned from Whistler--he said, "I build the form and destroy it. I build the form and I destory it. I build it and I destroy it." By going all those different processes you have got a piece of artwork the only thing that can copy that is a digital camera. You know, a human effort would be totally impossible and that ends up being the beauty. And these people that lay down the same brush stroke next to the same brushstroke, next to the same brushstroke and they are doing it over and over. They are going "Oh boy! Man, I just think this brushwork looks really beautiful!" and they won't ever touch it. Well you know, if you think about it, the logical conclusion to brushwork is when you start the painting, neutralize the brushwork as much as you can in the beginning and then when you go to the centrality of focus and you're going to tell your story and you are going to make this thing happen. That is when it gets happy and that is when you start making registrations that count. But if you get too many registrations that start to count in the beginning, the only way you can conclude that painting is to go to rendering. And how many of us want to sit down and render?

Linda: No thanks.

Blanche: I think that is something that happens to everyone though. You're painting.
You are beginning to like it. Then it becomes too precious.

CW: Oh Yeah!

Blanche: And you become afraid to get a little loose with it once you start liking it too much.

CW: Everyone has to graduate into different experiences. Sometimes you have to be told and sometimes you don't have to be told. Sometimes it is just looking at it and seeing it but if you control everything with so much-so deliberately, you can end up with a very unmoving static piece of artwork and that type of artwork doesn't really give the audience a chance to participate because it doesn't have something poetic. That is why poetry is some the finest literature out there because it is so poetic and people can put their lives into it because it is open for that. But the minute you close the door and become so literal that closes out your audience because there is only a certain brand of people that want to participate with that. That is what is so beautiful about impressionism it is the most revered art form because it is the most poetic out there and leaves a lot more room for interpretation. You've got a lot larger audience.

Linda: Absolutely.

Blanche: That's good advice.

Linda: Let's talk…move into the Weekend With the Masters--Your workshops there. How many WWM have you done, CW?

CW: I've done 2. I did the one in..the first one was down at Dana Point and then we did Monterey last year and then this year down in San Diego.

Linda: If there is one thing you can, it is probably what you were just telling us, but I'll ask anyway, what is the one thing, if you could instill one thing, in your students after they leave your workshop, what would that be?

CW: All of the above!

Linda: (laughing) That is what I thought you were going to say.

CW: All of the above. There is no need to go over all of that. That's really the nuts and bolts of it. People are so worried "Gee I really want to find my voice." And I say "Well you know what you need to learn is how to paint first." Here's the deal you have to become a painter before you become an artist. You know they want to be artists. You watch American Idol--I love the program and they say "Well my parents say I'm great." Well. They have no education. They haven't studied voice. They haven't trained their voice and haven't done any studying or anything and they just sing. It's the same thing--you have to know the science before you can really become an "artist" and graduate into it. Because a painter needs to know how to copy the subject, copy value, copy the edges, make the head look like a human head and not a dinosaur, the list goes on and on. Those are all the things you have to accomplish before you graduate into an artist. You have to become a painter first because you have to learn how to understand your craft. Once you understand the craft then you can quickly graduate into becoming an artist because if a lot of people end up in the business, ended up staying being a painter they are not an artist at all. They are still a painter. They are still--trapped into to it--like what George Gallo said-- you know there are certain things you cannot copy. The landscape, for example and make it as beautiful as it is because God did that. It's tough. It is totally impossible. But what you can do is put you personality and your slant of what that landscape means to you and then be creative and tweak it and move a tree like Edgar Payne says in his design book. If you got to move a rock or tree, don't be an idiot, move it if it is going to make a better design, you have to pay the dues and then once you realize and really know the craft and you've got a certain amount of experience in that, then you graduate and then you become an artist. A painter is not a means to an end. We don't need a lot more painters out there, what we need are a lot more people that are really artists. It is a real journey to become an artist. You know and I'm still becoming an artist. Thank God!

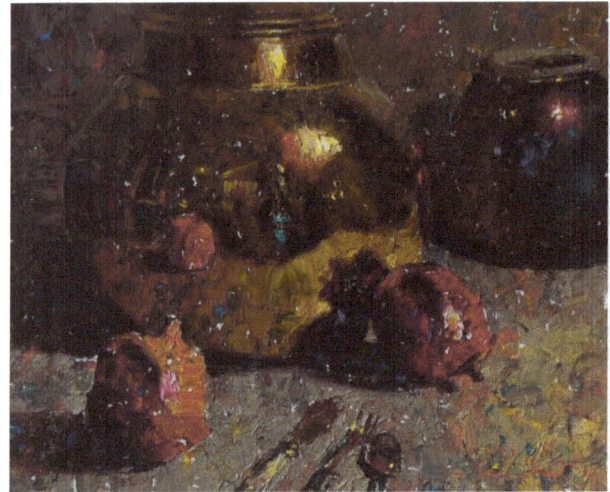

2011 Pomegranates With Brass 16x20 ©CWMundy

Blanche: To create versus rather than replicate the scene?

CW: You want to get to that. If that is a means to the end and that is what some of the ultra-conservative people who are out there in the business and there are a lot of those that are brand names too and they think you are knocking the doors down if you can do a great job copying that and that's just a beginning. Are you going to be a slave to copying the value, slave to copying the edges slave to copying the color, a slave to copying the subject? God gave us a brain and gave us the right and left hemisphere. Use them! Use the left hemisphere to solve your problems. And then use the right side to be creative. That is what the audience wants. They want to see like what Carolyn Anderson said "I've seen that before. Show me something I haven't seen.", and then that is when you are really starting to cut the mustard. And there is still so much room for somebody to come into the industry to give us a different attitude and a different look at that. But if you are going to stay in that zone and just think you are cutting the mustard because you can really do a great job of copying, I just kind of feel sorry for those people because they missed the whole point. Art is a big, big, big, big, BIG, BIG World. And high art is even bigger. There is no reason why all of us can't get in the position to create high art. We've just got to take the science and start letting people know who you are and it is your lifetime. It's the whole experience. It is everything all wrapped up in that paint brush, the towel, the palette knife, whatever you are making marks with on the canvas. You can end up making yourself vulnerable to the public and that is what the public wants. They--the collectors-- are out there just waiting to put that money down on your painting.

Linda: I wanted to –there is a lady by the name of Johanna Harmon who is in the chat room who is listening to us live and she wanted me to thank you, CW, for reminding everyone to be fearless.

CW: I love her...Johanna called me up one time because we--she took my en plein Masters in Europe, she took a photograph of me with my billybob teeth and my guitars. She asked if she could put it on the internet and I said sure--if I can't laugh at myself and I look pretty goofy and (does the theme from *Deliverance*) so anyway. Tell you what--there's a girl--a prime example that goes and studies with people and I don't mean me and yeah she studies with me and hopefully I helped her. She studied with Gerhartz and other artists and look what she is able to paint she is a very, very good artist. She isn't a painter she is an artist. And she is really producing great work and what she said about being fearless. The more that you take on that attitude and are willing to take chances and find out how far left is and how far right is, you are going to move up the food chain in the industry a lot quicker.

Linda: She just typed "Yes, you helped me."

CW: She's just a dear. Now she is a brand name in the industry. She won major awards.

Linda: She also wanted to know..she wanted to ask you who you think the most poetic living artist is?

CW: You know I'd have to sit down and think about that. I think the answer is not who is, of course, I know it would be a neat thing to name them, but then on one day I might say it is this person another day I might say it is another person, but I think more importantly is just ask yourself, "How can I be that poetic living artist?". You know George Gallo--I'll tell you a story George told me that just proves my point. And man, am I so grateful that he told me. We were up at Weekend With the Masters up in Monterey and we are having some great conversations and George says: "I had this French girlfriend when I was a young painter and we were having a couple glasses of wine and I was fixing dinner and I had her look at my painting." and he said, "So what do you think?" She looks at the painting and then she looks back at George. She looks back at the painting. She looks at George. Then she looks at the painting again for a minute. She looks at George and he goes "Well? What do you think?" She goes "George?" He goes, "Yeah!" She says, "No mystery" (laughs) and that's my point. That is when I think he-George-had a major epiphany because I'm sure they discussed that and she explained if you tell everybody way too much and give them too much information. I'm being too literal, you look at it and you walk on because you get the message and that's it but if there is mystery well is that a palette knife rock or is that a ship in the distance or what is that? You know, a photographer told me one time, a very good photographer said, look at photographs that have things in there that you can't really figure out. If you look at A. Zorn he has these abstract Dali thing going on in the back ground and you don't know if it is a coffee pot percolator or what everything is but it has shape and it is abstract but it makes you stop-it is another element of the painting that makes you want to look at it longer and see if you can figure that out. That was a great thing that George Gallo shared with me and I told my students and I shared that with the audience here today. You need some mystery in your work. You know guys, you want to be somebody that is cutting the mustard, man, get some mystery in there.

Blanche: That is a good story. CW in your workshop at Weekend With the Masters you are going to be teaching/painting still life and talking about the science of the painting which we sort of been talking about for few minutes. Tell us about the seven foundation truths.

CW: Well, first of all, I came up with the number seven because it is a Biblical number and that spiritually this is the most important thing to me: is my relationship with the Lord. The painting is just away to provide for my family and missions and for people who need help and things like that. That is what really makes me tick. Let's see--I got off on a tangent--what was the question again?

Blanche: Tell us a little about the seven foundation truths.

CW: Seven is an important Biblical number but I--also equally important--I boiled it down to seven tenants what I call the architecture of painting, and that is drawing, squinting, design value, color, edges and paint manipulation. Then I go on with talking about variety and then I go and talk about unity in each one of the disciplines and then I go and talk about the alien factor, association factor and the face factor. Those are all three element that are very crucial in painting.

Blanche: We've just been talking and we've already talked about the interview with George Gallo and us being a director of our painting. Does your directorship of painting discuss design or does it touch on all the elements from the start to finish of the painting?

CW: Well I talk about all--I discuss in great detail--now Weekend With the Masters because they will only be with me for a day--you can only give them a thumbnail and that thumbnail is when you try to give the most important stuff that you can but it is an encouragement for them if they really want to get down to business then they come and take your class for a week. And then I really am a stickler talking about the directorship and taking serious responsibility that we need to take in authoring the work. You need to be that director and not falling asleep in the director's chair. One of the key things I discuss in my workshops is the thing--one of the greatest things that I gleaned from Dan Gerhartz. I'd had a Master's degree and a teaching degree in art and study with great painters but nobody ever told me to solve all your problems upfront before you ever dip the brush and that came from Gerhartz and there is not a smarter thing to point out and that is where the directorship comes in. In fact your subject is your enemy to start out and then it ends up being your best friend. If you do what you wanted to do and do it with great directorship you know that is just the way it is.

Linda: I'm going to ask you two more questions on art, we are coming up an hour and have 90 minutes scheduled and I want to get to your music. These are the final two questions we are going to ask on art. Then we are going to switch over to your musical pursuits. Susan from AIS wanted to know what kind of brushes and palette knifes you use?

CW: Well my students come to my workshops and they've got these little knick knack paddy whack palette knives that are half an inch by a quarter of an inch and I don't know what they are good for-would probably be good if you are going to do a panting an inch by an inch maybe but I tell them those things need to hit the waste basket. I like the ones that are about an inch and quarter that are rounded on the tips, rounded on the sides and I like the larger ones. I use different sizes for different needs. Just like I said, sometimes I'm a one ply Kleenex and sometimes I'm a two ply. The one ply is for real intricate strategic stuff that you don't want to move around paint as much and then the two ply is for, you know you really want to molest the surface of the painting. Palette knives, it comes with experience and you find out what works best for you. The instrument is a lot more important for putting paint on and putting it on like cake frosting. People think they are really cutting mustard. There is a lot that the pallete knife will do—you can skip over spots and you can load it up, you can load up the palette knife with a lot of marbleized paint, improvising and get a lot more bang for your buck on the canvas. I forget who the great master was but he said; really what happens the best painting that they got is not the one the is finished that are hanging on the wall, but the best painting is their palette. And that's another thing about being bold, like what Johanna was saying, being bold and being out there. Get some stuff up there on the canvas that you might not normally do. You know you can control it. You can always back it down a little bit if it too garish or too gaudy or if it is causing a problem, but you ought to do some mixing on your canvas instead of mixing all paint down there. You might find out that you have a lot more interesting painting. Paint brushes-- I love Rosemary Brushes--The lady from England. Matt Smith taught me use the natural mongoose. I saw him painting how beautifully he painted those paintings and I was using pig bristle. Now pig bristle has a real point to it if you want to leave grooves in your paint that is a really wonderful instrument to do that. The natural mongoose will give you less striation in the paint and have a whole different feel.

Linda; I love mongoose.

CW: I use to use the short flat. The first time I used a long Rosemary flat I called this artist buddy of mine that I paint with a lot, Tom Reifers who lives in Indianapolis, a very good painter. I called him up and I said "You got to try these Rosemary brushes--the long flats." and he goes "Oh yeah really?" I said "Yeah man I started painting with it and I hated it when I started off." He said "Oh really? Why is that?" and I said "It was like using a mop!" and then I said "And then I got to the point where I liked the mop instead of the short flats." And then another thing I was out painting with Robert Gruppe who is the son of the famous Emile Gruppe in Gloucester and I noticed he used a lot of rounds and I thought--*hello idiot-this is why they look the way they look.* You like what Robert is doing. Why don't you use some rounds? So these last two paintings I used some flats. The flat has its purpose and the purpose will be unique to the artist there is no formula. And the round, think about it, the rounds, you can put that registration down and when you pull it off, guess what, it comes to a really beautiful point. Isn't that wonderful? Or you can mash it down and it will come to a round instead of a chisel. Everybody thinks Well I've gotta use the flat cause I want that chiseled look like Clyde Aspevig gets with his painting.

And believe me, they are beautiful and I don't know anybody who paints those snow scenes better than him. Edgar Payne didn't paint them as beautiful as Clyde painted, but that is what that brush will do but you got to be careful or everything will be chiseled. Hello! So you know using a variety of different marks on your canvas, those rounds, and you can scumble with them. You can mash them down like you mash the flats down but I really like it because this stuff that I got with Sherrie McGraw with getting beautiful, graceful form; I hope you people out there that are listening to this interview will get Sherrie McGraw's book on, it's called *"The Language of Drawing from an Artist's Viewpoint"*--get that and read it. It is a real easy, quick read. It is just unbelievable. And she has just a beautiful, graceful look to her drawings and her work and her painting and even though I want to be the molestation king and you know, really mess up the painting and lose edges I can still have beautiful, graceful form, can't I? That is something that I had to say because I got that from her. And again this is a great plug for her because she is so deserving. It will change your life. The girl knows what she's doing.

Blanche: There is going to be a big run on her books tonight.

CW: That is good!! I'm telling you what, man, I know what I'm talking about! I have a very good eye for great art because I had a great education. I just can't paint that way yet. But I'm on my way. I think I'm a good artist, I'm not a great artist, but I'm a good artist, but you know what if I keep learning like I'm learning and still have the passion, I think someday I could be a great artist and I would say that about everybody else out there. That's not an egotistical statement I hope people don't take it that way. I mean that is my goal. I want to be-I would like to be a great artist. And it takes a lot of work and it takes a lot of understanding but thank God we got people in the industry like Carolyn Anderson, Dan Gerhartz , Quang Ho , Kevin Macpherson, Clyde Aspevig, Richard Schmid, Scott Burdick, and Sue Lyons. I could just keep going on and on. These people know a lot and when you see something you like about that find out what it is and see how you can put a twist on that and use it in your work because don't just copy their style. That is where a lot of people get misled. They think, if I can paint like Richard Schmid then I'll be in the Putney Painters, boy! I'll just be cutting the mustard. Richard doesn't want you to paint just like him. He wants you to have your own brain just learn what he is doing and find a way to twist it. Take his visual language and make it unique to you. So anyway I'm going off on tangents.

Linda: What I'm going to do now, CW, is start *"Door County Cove"* song and then I'll turn the volume down and I want you to talk to us while it is playing in the background. You know, about your journey in making music. So let me start *"Door County Cove"*.

(Music Starts Playing)

CW: This is a project that I wanted to do for a long time. I played professionally out in LA, played in Las Vegas, I played with the Harry James band, Phil Harris, Frank Sinatra Jr. at the famous Frontier Hotel, so I have a lot of history in music. At one time I wanted that to be my career, but Thank God, He brought that to an end. The girl that was in our major band we were getting ready to sign with MCA , who had just taken on Elton John. They were making us the next Nitty Gritty Dirt Band because we wrote all our own songs and we were an acoustical show band. But our fiddle player was dying of Hodgkin's Disease and she came back from Stanford from a chemotherapy treatment and she had pretty much lost her mind and that was the end of that, They had to take her back to France. And she passed away. That was that end of that But God told me, you know, I 'm going to have you do artwork and you are going to go back to your first love and music is not going to be your career and I'm so grateful because this way I didn't have to depend on a lot of other people. I just have to depend on my relationship with the Lord and my wife and my painting. But the music has always been a big love of mine and so it was time for me to put down tracks a cd of all my original music and that is what I did.

Blanche: Do you think the creative process is the same between creating music and creating art?

CW: It's all the same thing. You have to become a musician before you become an artist. You have to become a painter before you become an artist. It's all about rhythm. It's all about movement. It's all about mood. It's all about personality. It's all about poetry. It's all about all the same things. You know, audibly, there's a lot of relationships that happen to the ear which is one of the five senses, and what happens to the eyes, which is another one of the five senses. So, ah, it's really pretty much all the same you know. You can have a song that has a chorus because they have a climatic point that they can return to and then they have verses. It is the same with a painting. You have a centrality of focus and then you have the supporting cast, which are the verses. And then you have the tertiaries in your painting which cannot battle and be more important than the secondary and it is the same thing with music. You got the bass player playing at the right volume and the drummer playing at the right volume so he's not obnoxiously running over the guy playing lead or whoever is singing. It's all the same stuff. It's the same thing with dance, same thing with music. All the arts they are all the same.

Blanche: Have a question here from Dwayne who is with the American Impressionist Society. He wanted me to ask what kind of banjo you play?

CW: I'm so blessed I got my buddy, Steve Huber, who lives in Nashville Tennessee, and in my estimation and I think many other people who are banjo players in the industry think he is making one of the finest banjos out there in the industry. By trade he is an engineer, so he has done things with the electronics, the mics, to get the same vibration that a prewar tone ring that will go on a Gibson, a prewar Gibson banjo and the rim—the wood rim which is maple and get the same vibrations that those produce and manufactured that, electronically, to get the banjo to have the same sound. And I think for my money he's probably got the closest you are going to get to a prewar banjo sound that is out there. There are other people who are on the same quest and they do a nice job too and I don't want to step on their toes. But Huber has done one of the most outstanding jobs with that. If you think about it, you can spend 5 or 6000 dollars to get a killer beautiful looking, great sounding banjo, instead of having to spending 75 to100-150-

250,000 dollars to get a prewar master tone. So he has a real place in the market and couldn't happen to a nicer guy. Steve is one of the finest banjo players out there in the industry.

Blanche: We also have another cut from your cd, called *"Road to Damascus"*. Let's listen to that for a little bit...

CW: Road to Damascus is the Biblical story of Saul, who was out to kill and destroy as many Christians as he could and he was on the road to Damascus to kill a few more and the apparition of Christ knocked him off his horse and he became Paul, one of the greatest living apostles to write some of the greatest epistles in the New Testament ever written, so it is that most important story of Saul becoming Apostle Paul and instead of killing Christians trying to minister to them through the word that the Holy Spirit gave him. So that is why it is called *"Road to Damascus"*. The reason I wanted you to play the fiddle section, I wanted people to know out there that this cd is not just about CW Mundy. Yes, I wrote the music and directed it, but I have some of the finest musicians in all of Nashville that are, Thank God, friends of mine. They played on this cd and the whole thing about that cd was I wanted to produce a piece of art. I didn't want to produce just a regular 1 4 5 bluegrass cd that so many of the bluegrassers are doing, because I love jazz and swing and contemporary bluegrass and a lot of other music. I grew up with the big band sound, Tommy Dorsey and others like that, that my parents played all the time. So I like a lot of music. It was just time for me to, my wife agreed, so we spent the money to produce songs that I had written and then I was the director and I was able to get one of the greatest engineers in the industry Scott Vestal. Scott is probably, by most banjo players will agree with this, in the industry, one of the finest if not the greatest living banjo players and he is equally a genius at engineering. So I knew I wanted to bring Scott in on the project because Scott and I are good friends and he did a masterful job. It's like I said about the directorship. I could have great players and all that and have pretty good songs but if he doesn't spin it right, and record it right and mix it right, then I got nothing. And that is one of the great things that people comment about the cd—there is not a blemish on the cd—well maybe my playing (chuckles) but everything else—it's just a brilliant piece of artwork and I know people might think—"Well he is proud of himself"- and I don't mean to sound that way. But it is really engineered phenomenally. And I've got some of the greatest living musician-bluegrass musicians that are out there that are all playing on the cd. And I told them that it was going to be an art project and they were excited that it wasn't just another bluegrass cd because when they get called in on session, they got to do the straight away bluegrass and they don't get to be as creative. But this I told them "Look, I'm having you guys be a part of this project because you know a lot more than I do and I want to make sure that you put that in there on the cd, because I'm not capable of it." So it really turned out to be a real exciting project and we are so grateful for it. I designed all the album cover-cd cover all the inside and everything and I designed that. And it makes really good coasters for wet drinks like Coke-Cola and stuff like that.
(Laughter)

Blanche: Now that we've heard a little bit of cd, I think there will be a lot of people looking for that tonight maybe on Amazon. It is called Road Trip.

CW: Thank you, I think it is really worth their money. It is really a compilation. There is one song on there that I wrote when my wife Rebecca, my Mother in Law and Father in Law, we took a cruise down the Amazon and we were in Brazil and the cruise ship pulled up to the spot and there were these loud speakers going on and it was that Latin Pop with the techno-drums and a little bit of the rap going on with the lead vocals and this driving and bouncing and I just loved it! And it has that light island techno sound to it. So I put one of those in there too because it is part of my road trip. My life is out on the road. My wife and I spend a lot of time going to a lot of places and that is one of the reason it was titled Road Trip and then the other reason is people could put it in their cd player when they are driving down the road and if they want to have time pass by they can turn it up loud or turn it down low and just have it as background and have a conversation.

Linda: Ok we are down to about 13 minutes left. Blanche—do you have one last question that you'd like to ask CW?

Blanche: Let's see, when you paint plein air, how do you decide on the theme to paint. When I get out there in the great outdoors, I get overwhelmed by all there is around me. Do you have a set of questions you ask yourself to try and narrow down what would be interesting to paint?

CW: I said on one of catalogs, that was a whole compilation of painting over in Europe, I said, what was the phrase, "Many scenes grab me, but a few are chosen."   And I think that comes with experience and I tell my students it takes real experience—not just an experienced painter but an experienced artist to know what will translate. You'd be amazed and I'm sure it happens to you girls too and the audience their neighbor or their parents or their grandparents go "Oh such and such…you ought to see this scene. It's the most beautiful thing—you should really paint it" (laughter) and you go look at it and it is six million trees and an overlook and the sky. Well you better be a real genius and a unbelievable artist to paint that and to make it worthy or it will be nothing. A subject matter will have enough hallmarks in it that will translate that will give you enough light dark pattern-shadow pattern and design that will really beckon you to paint it. I want the subject to tell me-"you cannot walk away and not paint me. You cannot walk away and not paint me." And when I hear that coming into my head—guess what? I get the stuff out and solve the problems have an understanding of what I am doing and how I want it to look and what I want to do to it. And you know what is amazing, it's kind of like what Michael Jordan was showing the audience in the playoffs when he runs by the scorer's bench and throws up his hands and goes "Well, what can I say?" You know everything he is shooting is going in. You see what I mean? It's the same thing with your painting. If you really solve the problems and have an understanding of what you need to do to attack that canvas it's like the painting paints itself. And I have had several times, believe me, when the Lord says "You're done" And I'm going "No I'm having too much fun. Let me try this" and he goes "You're done." And Carolyn Anderson will tell you that you get a painting to a certain point and there are a lot of different conclusions you can come up with it just depends what conclusion you want to go with. Now it takes a seasoned artist to understand that. But that is where she is at, because believe me, she is a very seasoned artist and one of my all-time favorite friends and one of my all-time favorite figure painters. There is nobody more poetic with the head and figure than Carolyn. She trumps everybody. I love Quang Ho's figure work. I love Dan Gerhartz and I love Richard Schmid, Sue Lyons, Sherrie McGraw, David Leffel, but for the real shorthand of the head and figure and only putting in the essentials and making it poetic, for my money there is nobody better than Carolyn.

Blanche: Well that is something to know when to stop.

CW: Yes—it takes a seasoned artist to understand that. But there are times when even though you know should stop don't smack your hands because you are going to go, "I'm going to try this or I'm still going to try that." Hey-you are never going to know how far right and left is unless you go out on that limb.

Linda: If you are interested in purchasing Road Trip, you can go out to CW website, www.cwmundy.com, and he has a Music tab up at the top. Just click on that and there are places there where you can buy his cd. And if you just click on one of the icons there, like one is CDBaby, Amazon and a few other places. You go right to the site to the spot where Road Trip is listed and you can purchase it there. We are going to end with one of CW's other songs this evening called "Moon Surf" and CW this is your opportunity to talk about this song and leave us with some parting wisdom.

CW: There are a couple things I'd like to say before you start this up if it is ok with you girls?

Blanche and Linda: Sure. That's fine.

CW: I'd like a little closer on this interview. First, of all, what I would like to say is that I can't tell you how honored my wife and I are that you guys, would think it would be important to have me on your program. I am very very honored and I take it as a great honor and privilege to do this. I hold it as a great honor and responsibility to speak to the artists and to try and give them hope and encourage. That is my gift. The gift that God has given me. That gift of exhortation. My students all know that. And for you that are listening that don't know me as a person that is what I'm all about. I also want to say too that I hope that I haven't come off arrogant, I will admit that I am opinionated and I think you'll find out that some of the better painters in this country and around the world are very opinionated. I am opinionated, but I have a lot of experience to base that opinion on. I don't want to come across arrogant, and I apologize to anybody if I seem to be arrogant because I don't like arrogant people and I don't want to come off sounding arrogant. I am confident but I also want to tell all you artists out there, that there is a lot that CW Mundy can learn and I learn it from looking at my peers and from looking at the history of art. There is always something out there that is inspiring to me and that's what keeps that passion going. Because I can promise you artists out there, if I don't have any passion toward what I'm doing, I don't even pick up the paint brush. Don't even think about trying to paint if you don't have the excitement or thrill, because your painting will be dead as a doornail and won't have anything going for it. You have to find out how you can incorporate passion and have that passion and if you got that passion. People have ask me about, "Gee if people are just born with all this really great talent?" And I go, No, it's like what Bob Knight told me, I was his first artist illustrator and it is all about preparation. It's all about persistence. It's all about the work ethic. It's all about the excitement and the drive that will keep you sustained. Like I said, it is one thing to launch your career and it is another thing to sustain it. If you don't have the passion, I can tell you in a heartbeat it won't take your collectors very long to figure out that his pen is empty. He doesn't have anything else to say. And so I just wanted to close with that, because I take this—I'm dead serious about this-and as Johanna knows and some of the other listeners know me as a person, I'm a joker and I'm dead serious—I'm both. I can laugh and cry at the same time. I'm very excited that I had an opportunity to do this. I hope that it is inspirational to you people to be brave and bold and work your butt off and you'll be amazed at what you'll accomplish.

Linda: CW, I speak for Blanche here as well. We are very honored that you would come on our little show and I'm looking forward meeting you in person in San Diego. We hope that you'll come back on our show again.

CW: Hey, I'd love to man! People that know me well, I'm not anybody who is short of words. They have to kind of tell me to shut me up. Like I said, if I talk to long you got to bust in there and say, ok, let's go on to the next subject.

Linda: Ok, I'm going to start "Moon Surf" now, because we are running out of time. I want to get most of this song in here.

Linda: This song reminds me of when I was on an Alaskan cruise and I can almost hear like whale sounds. I mean, it is beautiful.

Blanche: It is beautiful.

CW: It is a very moody piece. Moody art is some of the most beautiful art ever produced I think.

Linda: We are about ready to go off the air. So thank you everyone for tuning in and thank you CW!

CW: Thank you girls and have a great evening and the audience as well.

Blanche: Good night!

Linda: You too! Goodnight everyone!

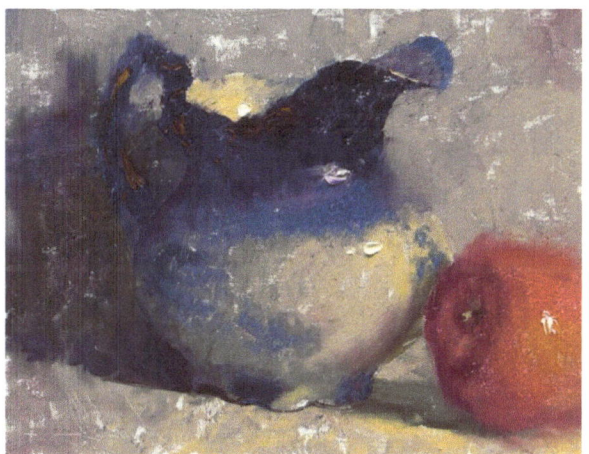

2011 - Favorite Pitcher, oil on linen, 9x12 ©CWMundy
Sold through Windows to The Divine Invitational Exhibition, Madden Museum, Greenwood Village, Colorado

In Closing:

This interview was so inspiring to me personally and in a way set me free. You see, I was worrying way too much about the technical stuff. So much so that I couldn't put a mark on the canvas without studying it, scrutinizing it, painfully eyeing it until I took myself to paralysis. It wasn't fun anymore. I wanted so badly to be an artist!! I wasn't allowing myself to make mistakes. Since my expectations were so high, I thought that if it wasn't a perfect piece of artwork then I somehow let my viewers down.

CW, through this interview, had given me permission to explore and….wait for it…even fail! So what if what I did was not perfect. Put the registrations down and build the painting. Don't be afraid to ask yourself, "What if I do this here—in this precious little area that I love so much?" Destroy it! Challenge yourself to find a way to rebuild it. Mess it up! Use tools you may never had thought of using before.

And so I did! The result has been a bigger leap in my learning then in the previous five years. While everyone loves the acceptance and praises they receive for their beautiful artwork, that no longer keeps me from destroying the precious areas because sometimes, not all the time, but sometimes those precious areas are what is wrong with the painting. As a matter of fact, if something is too precious in my painting, the palette knife comes out and away it goes. I force myself to make it precious again and fit into the larger painting.

So, how does one do this and yet get out of the way of the painting? Never allow your conscious self to latch on to any part of the painting until it is a whole, complete painting. If I find myself liking one area way too much, I've entered into the painting process. I'm no longer hanging out on that limb. Let go of the ownership.

If you have had the opportunity to watch CW paint then you know he prays over his paints and canvas before he starts. If you listen closely to his words, he asks for guidance and for God to work through CW in the execution of his art. In this way, CW is taking himself out of the way and allowing it to happen. This is CW's way and you will, over time, find the way that bests takes you out of the process. It all comes down to trust. Do you trust that you are an artist? Do you trust that you are capable of creating a beautiful work of art? Do you trust that you have studied and worked hard? If you answered yes, then let go of your conscious self and allow it to happen.   Just have fun throwing paint around and see what happens at the end. The control freak in us can always fix it. And so what if we can't!! At least we learned from it, right?

I had always wanted to paint this painting. It is the TSS Earnslaw, a streamer that sails Lake Wakatipu in Queenstown, New Zealand. Every morning while visiting there, she would get that smoke billowing from her stack, toot the whistle and then head down the lake to Walter Peak. I had seen a number of paintings of this steamship and wonderful photos too. It had so many intricate details, corners,--it was just overwhelming to me.   After interviewing CW, I decided that the excuses of not painting something I wanted desperately to paint needed to be set aside.

Here's the painting…

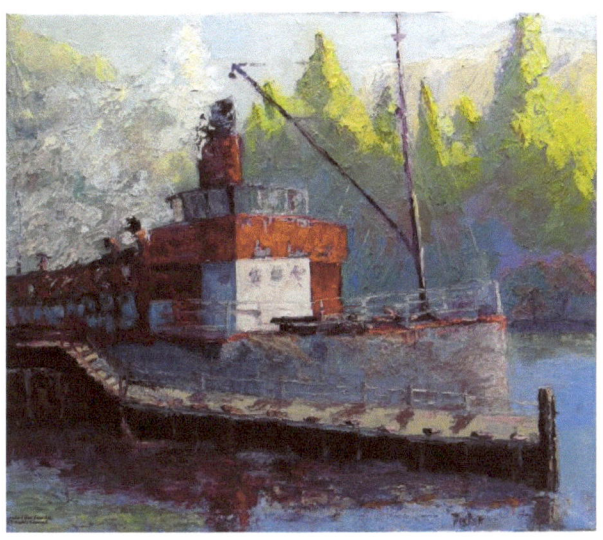

©Linda Riesenberg Fisler, TSS Earnslaw
20 x 24, Oil on Canvas (Personal Collection)

I'd like to take you through my personal journey of exploration on this painting. It started me down the path of exploring and painting for fun. The first thing I did was sketch this boat. Every overwhelming detail on the boat was questioned as to its need to be in the painting. Next, mini-composition sketches were drawn—not large just 1 inch by 1 inch squares. This helped me to decide to break out from my usual canvas size (16 x 20) to a larger canvas (20 x 24).   The best mini-comp I had down lent itself to this size. From there I started with a greyscale sketch on the canvas using an oversized bristle brush to accomplish what would be the position and value scale in the painting. No details were included, just large shapes. Next up, I grabbed a brush and put in shapes of color. As usual with my brush in hand, I immediately went to too much detail and felt defeated.

For some reason, palette knives provide me the freedom that I was looking for all this time. I'm not sure why, but they do and I don't feel a need to examine why. So after a few days of feeling defeated and wallowing in self-pity, I picked up the palette knife and destroyed the brushed on, too detailed shapes. I stopped painting trees, water, boat, pier and started playing with color (in the value range that I had previously set in my mind) and shapes of color all the while asking

"What if I do this?" "What color do I want here?" "Warmer? Cooler? Darker? Lighter?" It began to appear and I began to get out of its way.

The result was, well, you can see. And the best compliment of all? A comment on Facebook from the Master of boat painting himself—CW Mundy, who said: "Nice Work, Girl!"

That's all I needed to know I was on the right track again!

I hope this interview with CW and the comments made here will inspire you to free yourself and be fearless when you are painting. It is just so much fun!

With warm personal regards,

Linda Riesenberg Fisler

CW Mundy's website: http://www.cwmundy.com
Linda Riesenberg Fisler's website: http://www.lindafisler.com
Artist Mentor's Online (AMO) website: http://www.artistmentorsonline.com
Blanche McAlister Harris' website: http://www.blanchemcalisterharris.com
Barbara Coleman's website: http://www.barbaracoleman.com

www.ingramcontent.com/pod-product-compliance
Lightning Source LLC
Chambersburg PA
CBHW050428180526
45159CB00005B/2457